PLAYTIME RHYMES

THIS BOOK
BELONGS
TO

_____

_____

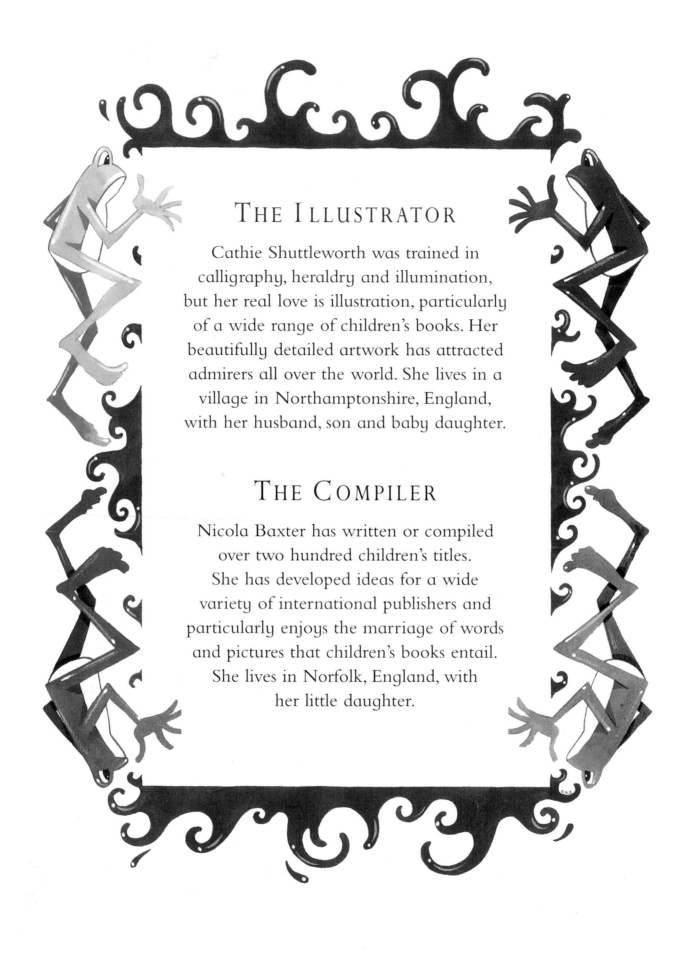

THE ILLUSTRATOR

Cathie Shuttleworth was trained in
calligraphy, heraldry and illumination,
but her real love is illustration, particularly
of a wide range of children's books. Her
beautifully detailed artwork has attracted
admirers all over the world. She lives in a
village in Northamptonshire, England,
with her husband, son and baby daughter.

THE COMPILER

Nicola Baxter has written or compiled
over two hundred children's titles.
She has developed ideas for a wide
variety of international publishers and
particularly enjoys the marriage of words
and pictures that children's books entail.
She lives in Norfolk, England, with
her little daughter.

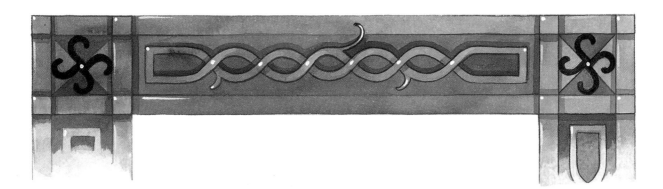

PLAYTIME RHYMES

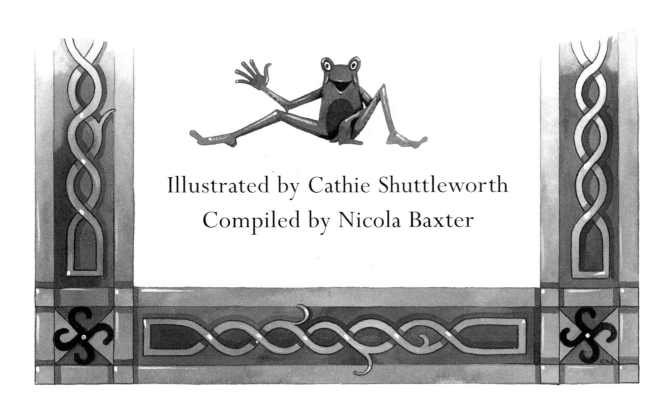

Illustrated by Cathie Shuttleworth
Compiled by Nicola Baxter

FOR JONAH SHRIVE
C.A.S.

Published by Armadillo Books
an imprint of Bookmart Limited
Registered Number 2372865
Trading as Bookmart Limited
Desford Road, Enderby
Leicester, LE9 5AD

ISBN 1-84322-013-X

Produced for Bookmart Limited by Nicola Baxter
PO Box 215, Framingham Earl Road, Norwich NR14 7UR

Designer: Amanda Hawkes
Production designer: Amy Barton
Editor: Sally Delaney

Printed in Singapore

CONTENTS

PLAYTIME RHYMES

Rhymes are fun for everyone. They're even better when there are actions to go with them. Here are rhymes to move about to, rhymes to wiggle your fingers to, rhymes that can go on and on, and rhymes where all your friends can join in. Have fun!

Five little hopping frogs
Sat on a spotted log
Wondering how to pass the time.
Yawn! Yawn!
One jumped into this book
And if you take a look
You'll see he has hopped into each rhyme!

Busy Bodies

Peter hammers with one hammer,
One hammer, one hammer,
Peter hammers with one hammer,
This fine day.
(Hammer with one fist.)

Peter hammers with two hammers…
(Hammer with two fists.)

Peter hammers with three hammers…
(Hammer with two fists and one foot.)

Peter hammers with four hammers…
(Hammer with two fists and two feet.)

Peter hammers with five hammers…
(Two fists, two feet and nod your head.)

Peter's very tired now… *(Head on hands.)*

Peter's fast asleep now… *(Quietly!)*

Peter's woken up now… *(Stretch!)*

8

What does the clock
in the hall say?
Tick ... Tock ... Tick ... Tock.

(Swing your arm like a pendulum.)

What does the clock
in the room say?
Tick-tock, tick-tock, tick-tock.

(Swing your hand as pendulum at twice the speed.)

What do all the little watches say?
Tickaticka tickaticka tickaticka tick!

(Wag your finger like a pendulum—very fast!)

9

I'm a little teapot, short and stout,
Here's my handle, here's my spout.
When I see the tea cups, hear me shout:
Tip me up and pour me out!

*(Hold your arms like a handle and a spout
and lean over sideways to pour!)*

10

Five fat sausages, sizzling in the pan.
One went pop!
And then it went BANG!

Four fat sausages, sizzling in the pan.
One went pop!
And then it went BANG!

Three fat sausages, sizzling in the pan.
One went pop!
And then it went BANG!

Two fat sausages, sizzling in the pan.
One went pop!
And then it went BANG!

One fat sausage, sizzling in the pan.
It went pop!
And then it went BANG!

(Pretend to be frying sausages. Open your fingers wide for "pop!" and clap your hands together for "BANG!")

11

Teddy bear, teddy bear, stand on tiptoes.
Teddy bear, teddy bear, touch your nose.
Teddy bear, teddy bear, nod your head.
Teddy bear, teddy bear, go to bed.
Teddy bear, teddy bear, wake up now.
Teddy bear, teddy bear, take a bow.
Teddy bear, teddy bear, turn around.
Teddy bear, teddy bear, touch the ground.
Teddy bear, teddy bear, show your shoe.
Teddy bear, teddy bear, that will do.
Teddy bear, teddy bear, climb the stairs.
Teddy bear, teddy bear, say your prayers.
Teddy bear, teddy bear, turn off the light.
Teddy bear, teddy bear, say goodnight.

*(Do all the actions that the teddy bear does, gradually
singing more softly as he gets ready for bed.)*

Row, row, row your boat
Gently down the stream.
Merrily, merrily, merrily, merrily,
Life is but a dream.

Rock, rock, rock your boat
Gently on the tide.
Merrily, merrily, merrily, merrily,
To the other side.

Row, row, row your boat
Gently down the stream.
But if you see a crocodile
Don't forget to scream!

*(Sit facing a partner and hold hands. Lean
forwards and backwards, then side to side—
and don't forget to scream at the end!)*

13

I went to visit a farm one day.
I saw a sheep across the way,
And what do you think I heard it say?
Baa, baa, baa!

I went to visit a farm one day.
I saw a cow across the way,
And what do you think I heard it say?
Moo, moo, moo!

I went to visit a farm one day.
I saw a duck across the way,
And what do you think I heard it say?
Quack, quack, quack!

I went to visit a farm one day.
I saw a dog across the way,
And what do you think I heard it say?
Woof, woof, woof!

14

I went to visit a farm one day.
I saw a cat across the way,
And what do you think I heard it say?
Mee-ow, mee-ow, mee-ow!

I went to visit a farm one day.
I saw a pig across the way,
And what do you think I heard it say?
Oink, oink, oink!

I went to visit a farm one day.
I saw a tractor across the way,
And what do you think I heard it say?
Brrrm, brrrm, brrrm!

(Pretend to be everything you see.)

15

Aeroplanes, aeroplanes, all in a row,
Aeroplanes, aeroplanes, ready to go.

(Kneel with arms outstretched.)

Hark, they're beginning
To buzz and to hum!

(Stand up but stay still.)

The engines are working,
So come along, come.

(Pretend to fly around the room.)

Now we are flying
High up in the sky,
Faster and faster,
Oh, ever so high.

(Bring aeroplanes in to land again.)

16

Here is the ostrich straight and tall,
Nodding his head above us all.

(Stretch arm above head.)

Here is the hedgehog prickly and small,
Rolling himself up into a ball.

(Fingers interlaced and sticking out, then closed.)

Here is the spider scuttling round,
Treading so lightly on the ground.

(Link thumbs, bend fingers down.)

Here are the birds that fly so high,
Spreading their wings across the sky.

(Link thumbs, spread fingers.)

Here are the children fast asleep,
Here at night the owls do peep.

(Make glasses around eyes with thumbtip and forefinger tip touching.)

17

(Chant slowly at first, getting faster and faster.)

I have a cat.

(Make whiskers with your fingers.)

And a bat

(Link thumbs and spread hands.)

And a tall, pointy hat.

(Indicate hat on head.)

I can brew a strange stew.

(Make a stirring action.)

I can tell you a spell.

(Point.)

I go ZOOM on my broom!

I'm a witch!

I wiggle my fingers
And I wiggle my toes,
I wiggle my shoulders
And I wiggle my nose.

Now all the wiggles
Are gone from me,
And I'm as still
As still can be.

19

I'm all made of hinges,
And everything bends,
From the top of my head,
To the tips of my ends.
I've hinges on the front,
And hinges behind,
If I didn't have hinges,
I couldn't unwind.

(Pretend to "wind up" the children first, then they can move stiffly, following the verse, like clockwork toys.)

20

Two little dicky-birds sitting on a wall,
One called Peter, one called Paul.
Fly away Peter, fly away Paul.
Come back Peter, come back Paul.

*(Use two fingers for birds and your opposite
forearm for the wall. Stick little scraps of paper on
your forefingers. Hide your fingers when the birds fly
away; then make them "fly" back onto the wall.)*

Stretch up high as tall as a house,
Curl up round and small as a mouse.
Now pretend you have a drum
And beat like this—tum, tum, tum.
Shake your fingers, stamp your feet,
Close your eyes and go to sleep.

I can tie my shoelace,
I can brush my hair,
I can wash my hands and face
And dress myself with care.

I can clean my teeth too,
And fasten shirts and frocks.
I can say "How do you do?"
And pull up both my socks!

*(Imitate the actions as you say them,
offering a hand to be shaken for "How
do you do?")*

23

Can you walk on tiptoe
As softly as a cat?
Can you stamp along the road
STAMP, STAMP, STAMP, like that?
Can you take some great big strides
Just like a giant can?
Or walk along so slowly
Like a bent old man?

24

Early in the morning,
(Rub your eyes.)

Down by the station,
(Point your finger.)

See the little engines
(Shade your eyes with your hand and look around.)

All in a row.
(Count with your fingers.)

See the engine driver
(Mime pulling down your cap.)

Blow on the whistle.
(Pretend to pull a handle to go "toot!")

Toot, toot!
Puff, puff!
And off we go!
(Make train wheel motions with your arms.)

An elephant walks like this and that,
(Lumber and sway.)
He's terribly tall and terribly fat.
(Show with hands.)
He hasn't any fingers,
(Wiggle fingers.)
He hasn't any toes
(Wiggle toes.)
But goodness gracious me,
Look at his nose!
(Make a trunk with your arm.)

Mix a pancake,
Stir a pancake,
Pop it in the pan.
Fry the pancake,
Toss the pancake,
Catch it if you can!

(Pretend to be holding a bowl full of mixture, pour it and then pretend to cook it and flip it in the pan.)

27

Here's a ball for baby,
Big and soft and round.

(Make ball shape with arms.)

Here is baby's hammer,
See how he can pound.

(Pretend to have a hammer.)

Here are baby's soldiers,
Standing in a row.

(Stand straight and to attention.)

Here is baby's music,
Clapping, clapping so.

(Pretend to be a conductor, then clap!)

Here's a big umbrella,
To keep the baby dry

(Make the shape of an umbrella with your arms.)

And here's the baby's cradle,
To rock a baby bye.

(Make a cradle with your arms and rock the baby.)

There's a wise old owl
Who has a pointy nose,
Two feathery ears
And claws on his toes.

He perches up high
And stares at you,
Then he opens his beak,
And cries, "Whoo-hoo!"

(Pretend to be like the owl,
using your body to sit like an
owl and your hands and fingers
to make a nose, ears, and so on.)

FINGER FUN

Five fat peas
In a peapod pressed,

(Hold up hand with fingers folded down.)

One grew, two grew,
And so did all the rest.

(Let fingers unfold.)

They grew and grew,
And did not stop,
They grew so fat,
The pod went POP!

(Clap hands.)

32

Here are the lady's knives and forks.
(Place hands back to back, pointing fingers upwards and interlacing them.)

Here is the lady's table.
(With fingers still interlaced, turn hands over so that the backs of your fingers make a table.)

Here is the lady's looking glass.
(Raise your little fingers.)

And here is the baby's cradle.
(Raise your index fingers and rock your hands.)

33

Tommy Thumb, Tommy Thumb,
Where are you?

(Hide your hands.)

Here I am, here I am,

(Give a thumbs-up sign.)

How do you do?

(Bend thumb as if bowing.)

Peter Pointer, Peter Pointer...

Toby Tall, Toby Tall...

Ruby Ring, Ruby Ring...

Baby Small, Baby Small...

*(Show index, middle, ring and little fingers in
turn as you complete each verse.)*

34

Up the tall white candlestick
Crept Mr. Mousey Brown
(Hold one arm upright and let the other hand
creep up it.)

Right to the top,
But he couldn't get down.
So he called to his Grandma,
"Grandma! Grandma!"
But Grandma was in town.
So he curled himself into a ball
And rolled right down.
(Make a fist and "tumble" it down your arm.)

Here you will find the deep blue sea
(Move your hand like waves.)

This is a boat
(Interlace your fingers, palms up.)

And this is me.
(Raise one thumb.)

All the little fishes down below
(Interlace your fingers, palms together.)

Waggle their tails and away they go!
(Wiggle your fingers and "swim" them away!)

Here is a tree with leaves so green

(Hold up your arms.)

Here are the apples
That hang between.

(Clench your fists.)

When the wind blows,
The apples will fall
Here is a basket to gather them all.

(Interlace your fingers, palms up.)

37

Roly poly e-ver so slow-ly
Roly poly ever so quick!

(Make a roly poly motion with your hands.)

Roly poly, roly poly,
Up, up, up!
Roly poly, roly poly,
Down, down, down!

(Hands up, then down.)

Roly poly, roly poly,
Out, out, out,
Roly poly, roly poly,
In, in, in.

(Hands out to the side, then in again.)

38

Roly poly, hands on your head,
Roly poly, hands behind your back,
Roly poly, hands on the floor,
(You can add as many lines to this as you like!)

Roly poly, roly poly,
Give a little clap,
Roly poly, roly poly,
Hands in your lap.

Wind the bobbin up,
Wind the bobbin up.
Pull, pull, clap, clap, clap!
Wind it back again,
Wind it back again,
Pull, pull, clap, clap, clap!

Point to the window,
Point to the floor,
Point to the ceiling,
Point to the door.

Wind the bobbin up,
Wind the bobbin up.
Pull, pull, clap, clap, clap!
Wind it back again,
Wind it back again,
Pull, pull, clap, clap, clap!

*(Roll hands over one another to wind the
bobbin up and back. Move fists away from one
another to pull.)*

40

Two snails from Wales
Went for a walk up a stalk,
Got to the top, couldn't stop.
Whoops!
They were found on the ground,
Two snails, back in Wales.

(Two fingers climb up the other arm and slide back down again.)

41

Five little ducks
(Hold up five fingers.)
Went swimming one day
(Make swimming movements with your hands.)
Over the hills and far away.
*(Make your hand swoop up and down in the
shape of hills.)*
Mother Duck said,
Quack, quack, quack, quack!
But only four little ducks came back.
(Hold up four fingers.)

Four little ducks
Went swimming one day
Over the hills and far away.
Mother Duck said,
Quack, quack, quack, quack!
But only three little ducks came back.

42

Two little ducks
Went swimming one day
Over the hills and far away.
Mother Duck said,
Quack, quack, quack, quack!
But only one little duck came back.

One little duck
Went swimming one day
Over the hills and far away.
Mother Duck said,
Quack, quack, quack, quack!
And all her five little ducks came back!

Two fat gentlemen met in a lane,
Bowed most politely,
Bowed once again.
"How do you do? How do you do?
How do you do?" again.
(Hold hands upright, palms facing,
fingers folded down, thumbs upright.
Dip thumbs as gentlemen bow.)

Two thin ladies met in a lane,
Bowed most politely,
Bowed once again.
"How do you do? How do you do?
How do you do?" again.

(Do the same with forefingers.)

Two tall policemen met in a lane,
Bowed most politely,
Bowed once again.
"How do you do? How do you do?
How do you do?" again.

(Middle fingers.)

44

Two big schoolboys met in a lane,
Bowed most politely,
Bowed once again.
"How do you do? How do you do?
How do you do?" again.

(Ring fingers.)

Two little babies met in a lane,
Bowed most politely,
Bowed once again.
"How do you do? How do you do?
How do you do?" again.

(Little fingers.)

45

Here's a church.

(Interlace fingers with knuckles up.)

Here's a steeple.

(Raise little fingers, tips touching.)

Open the doors...

(Open thumbs wide.)

And here are all the people!

(Turn hands over to show interlaced fingers.)

RHYMES WITHOUT END

The wheels on the bus
Go round and round,
Round and round, round and round,
The wheels on the bus
Go round and round,
All day long.
(Twirl both hands round and round.)

The bell on the bus
Goes ding, ding, ding,
Ding, ding, ding, ding, ding, ding,
The bell on the bus
Goes ding, ding, ding,
All day long.
(Pretend to press a button with one finger.)

The wipers on the bus
Go swish, swish, swish,
Swish, swish, swish, swish, swish, swish,
The wipers on the bus
Go swish, swish, swish,
All day long.
(Swish forearms from side to side.)

The daddies on the bus
Go snore, snore, snore,
Snore, snore, snore, snore, snore, snore,
The daddies on the bus
Go snore, snore, snore,
All day long.
*(Put your palms together, rest your
cheek on them and snore!)*

The mummies on the bus go chatter,
chatter, chatter,
Chatter, chatter, chatter, chatter,
chatter, chatter,
The mummies on the bus go chatter,
chatter, chatter,
All day long.
(Open and close hands like a talking mouth!)

The children on the bus bounce up
and down,
Up and down, up and down,
The children on the bus bounce up
and down,
All day long.
(Bounce up and down!)

The babies on the bus go waah,
waah, waah!
Waah, waah, waah, waah, waah,
waah!
The babies on the bus go waah,
waah, waah!
All day long!
(Pretend to be rocking a baby.)

The wheels on the bus
Go round and round,
Round and round, round and round,
The wheels on the bus
Go round and round,
All day long.
(Twirl both hands round and round.)

51

Here we go round the mulberry bush,
The mulberry bush, the mulberry bush!
Here we go round the mulberry bush,
On a cold and frosty morning!

This is the way we brush our hair,
Brush our hair, brush our hair.
This is the way we brush our hair,
On a cold and frosty morning.

Here we go round the mulberry bush…

This is the way we clean our teeth,
Clean our teeth, clean our teeth.
This is the way we clean our teeth,
On a cold and frosty morning.

Here we go round the mulberry bush…

This is the way we wash our faces,
Wash our faces, wash our faces.
This is the way we wash our faces,
On a cold and frosty morning.

Here we go round the mulberry bush…

This is the way we put on our clothes,
Put on our clothes, put on our clothes.
This is the way we put on our clothes,
On a cold and frosty morning.

Here we go round the mulberry bush…

This is the way we eat our breakfast,
Eat our breakfast, eat our breakfast.
This is the way we eat our breakfast,
On a cold and frosty morning.

(Hold hands and dance around in a circle for the chorus. Do actions for each verse and shiver in the last line. You could make up lots more verses!)

(Pretend to be each of these animals in turn.)

The hen has a chick
What does it say?
"Cheep, cheep, cheep, cheep!"
All through the day.

The duck has a duckling
What does it say?
"Quack, quack, quack, quack!"
All through the day.

The cow has a calf
What does it say?
"Moo, moo, moo, moo!"
All through the day.

The pig has a piglet
What does it say?
"Oink, oink, oink oink!"
All through the day.

The sheep has a lamb
What does it say?
"Baa, baa, baa, baa!"
All through the day.

The dog has a puppy
What does it say?
"Woof, woof, woof, woof!"
All through the day.

The cat has a kitten
What does it say?
"Me-ow, me-ow, me-ow, me-ow!"
All through the day.

I have a snail
What does it say?
It doesn't say anything
All through the day.

(Pretend to be all the animals on the farm.)

Old MacDonald had a farm,
Ee-aye-ee-aye-oh!
And on that farm
He had some pigs.
Ee-aye-ee-aye-oh!
With an oink, oink here,
And an oink, oink there,
Here an oink,
There an oink,
Everywhere an oink, oink!

Old MacDonald had a farm,
Ee-aye-ee-aye-oh!
And on that farm he had some hens…
With a cluck, cluck here…

Old MacDonald had a farm,
Ee-aye-ee-aye-oh!
And on that farm he had a dog…
With a woof, woof here…

56

Old MacDonald had a farm,
Ee-aye-ee-aye-oh!
And on that farm he had a tractor…
With a brrrm, brrrm here…

Old MacDonald had a farm,
Ee-aye-ee-aye-oh!
And on that farm he had a sheep…
With a baa, baa here…

Old MacDonald had a farm,
Ee-aye-ee-aye-oh!
And on that farm he had some cows…
With a moo, moo here…

(Add as many verses as you like!)

57

One finger, one thumb, keep moving,
One finger, one thumb, keep moving,
One finger, one thumb, keep moving,
We'll all be merry and bright.

One finger, one thumb, one arm,
    keep moving...

One finger, one thumb, one arm,
    one leg, keep moving...

One finger, one thumb, one arm,
    one leg, one nod of the head,
    keep moving...

One finger, one thumb, one arm,
    one leg, one nod of the head,
    stand up, sit down, keep moving...
(Imitate each action as described.)

If you're happy, you should show it,
Clap your hands!
If you're happy, you should show it,
Clap your hands!
If you're happy, you should show it,
Clap your hands and we'll all know it,
If you're happy, you should show it,
Clap your hands!

If you're happy, you should show it,
Wave your arms!

If you're happy, you should show it,
Turn around!

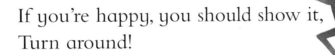

If you're happy, you should show it,
Take a bow!

If you're happy, you should show it,
Shout, "I am!"
(Carry out the actions and keep on adding more!)

Oh, I can play on the big base drum
And this is the music to it:
Boom, boom, boom goes the big
        base drum,
And that's the way to do it!

Oh, I can play on the triangle
And this is the music to it:
Ting, ting, ting goes the triangle,
And that's the way to do it!

Oh, I can play on the piano
And this is the music to it:
Tum, tumty, tum goes the piano,
And that's the way to do it!

*(Name as many more instruments as you can
and imitate their sounds. If several of you are
singing, finish with "Oh, I can play in an
orchestra" and all make different sounds!)*

ALL
TOGETHER
NOW!

Knock at the door!

(Tap child's forehead.)

Peep in!

(Touch eyelids.)

Lift the latch!

(Touch nose.)

Walk in!

(Pop finger in mouth.)

Take a chair!

(Pinch cheek.)

Sit there!

(Pinch other cheek.)

How do you do today, sir?

(Tickle under chin.)

62

Here sits the Lord Mayor

(Touch child's forehead.)

Here sit his men

(Gently touch eyes.)

Here sits the cockadoodle

(Touch right cheek.)

Here sits the hen

(Touch left cheek.)

Here sit the little chickens

(Touch nose.)

Here they run in

(Touch mouth.)

Chin chopper, chin chopper,
chin chopper chin.

(Tickle under chin.)

63

(Play this with four friends (or more, adding more verses!)

Five little froggies sitting on a well,
One looked up and down he fell;
Froggies jumped high
Froggies jumped low;
Four little froggies dancing to and fro.

Four little froggies sitting on a well,
One looked up and down he fell;
Froggies jumped high
Froggies jumped low;
Three little froggies dancing to and fro.

Three little froggies sitting on a well,
One looked up and down he fell;
Froggies jumped high
Froggies jumped low;
Two little froggies dancing to and fro.

Two little froggies sitting on a well,
One looked up and down he fell;
Froggies jumped high
Froggies jumped low;
One little froggy dancing to and fro.

One little froggy sitting on a well,
He looked up and down he fell;
Froggies jumped high
Froggies jumped low;
No little froggies dancing to and fro.

65

Jack-in-the-Box,
Quiet as a mouse,
Tucked way down inside his house.
There he lies, ever so still,
Will he come out?
Yes, he will!

(Children crouch down on the floor pretending to be the Jack-in-the-Box, jumping up at the last line.)

See the little bunnies sleeping
Though it's almost noon,
Shall I go and wake them
With a merry tune?
They're so still.
Are they ill?
Wake up, little bunnies!
Hop, little bunnies, hop, hop, hop!
Hop, little bunnies, hop, hop, hop!
Hop, little bunnies, hop, hop, hop!
Hop, hop, hop!

(Children lie down on the floor and keep as still as they can. When they are woken up, they hop up and down as vigorously as possible!)

(All join hands around the person chosen as the farmer and dance round as you sing:)

The farmer's in his den,
The farmer's in his den.
Ee-aye-addy-oh!
The farmer's in his den!

The farmer wants a wife,
The farmer wants a wife.
Ee-aye-addy-oh!
The farmer wants a wife!

(The farmer chooses a wife to join him in the circle.)

The wife wants a child,
The wife wants a child.
Ee-aye-addy-oh!
The wife wants a child!

(The wife chooses a child…)

68

The child wants a nurse,
The child wants a nurse.
Ee-aye-addy-oh!
The child wants a nurse!
(The child chooses a nurse…)

The nurse wants a dog,
The nurse wants a dog.
Ee-aye-addy-oh!
The nurse wants a dog!
(The nurse chooses a dog…)

The dog wants a bone,
The dog wants a bone.
Ee-aye-addy-oh!
The dog wants a bone!
(The dog chooses a bone…)

We all pat the dog,
We all pat the dog.
Ee-aye-addy-oh!
We all pat the dog!
(Everyone pats the dog!)

69

*(You can act this out with children
or toys on the floor.)*

There were five in the bed
And the little one said,
"Roll over! Roll over!"
So they all rolled over
And one fell out.

There were four in the bed...

There was one in the bed
And that little one said,
"Good, now I've got the bed to myself
I'm going to stretch … and stretch …
          and stretch!"

70

Father and mother and Uncle Bob
Went to the market on a cob.

(Child riding on both adult's knees.)

Father fell off!

(Drop left knee.)

Mother fell off!

(Drop right knee.)

But Uncle Bob went
jiggety-jiggety-jog!

An elephant went out to play
Upon a spider's web one day.
He found it such tremendous fun
He called another elephant to come.

Two elephants went out to play
Upon a spider's web one day.
They found it such tremendous fun
They called another elephant to come.

(And so on until…)

[Any number of] elephants
    went out to play
Upon a spider's web one day
The web went CREAK!
The web went CRACK!
And all of a sudden
They all ran back.

*(One child stands or dances in the middle of a
ring, with any number of elephants then called
in to join him.)*

Touch your head, shoulders,
Knees and toes (knees and toes).

Touch your head, shoulders,
Knees and toes (knees and toes).

And your eyes, your ears
Your mouth and nose.

Touch your head, your shoulders,
Knees and toes (knees and toes).

Head, shoulders, knees and toes,
Head, shoulders, knees and toes,
Eyes and ears and mouth and nose,
Head, shoulders, knees and toes.

(Do the actions, getting a little bit faster every time you sing or say the rhyme!)

73

(Children stand in a ring, holding hands when possible and follow the actions. To "do the hokey-cokey", clasp hands together and wiggle them from side to side.)

You put your left leg in,
Your left leg out,
In, out, in, out, shake it all about!
You do the hokey-cokey
And you turn around,
That's what it's all about.

(In the chorus, hold hands and rush towards the centre of the circle and back again as each line is sung. At the end, clap your hands above your head.)

Oh, oh the hokey-cokey!
Oh-oh the hokey-cokey!
Oh-oh the hokey-cokey!
Knees bend, arms raised,
Ra, ra, ra!

74

You put your right leg in…

You put your left arm in…

You put your right arm in…

You put your whole self in…
(Jump towards the centre and then jump backwards.)

(You can sing this song as a round to the tune of "Frère Jacques".)

I hear thunder, I hear thunder
Hark, don't you? Hark, don't you?

(Drum with hands or feet, or cup your hands to your ears.)

Pitter, patter raindrops,
Pitter, patter raindrops

(Flutter your fingers.)

I'm wet through.

(Stamp your feet and shake the rain off!)

So are you.

(Point to each other.)

76

I can nod my head
Like a little wooden puppet,
I can nod my head
Like a little wooden doll,
I can nod my head
Like a little wooden puppet,
I can nod my head
Like a little wooden doll.

I can walk up and down...

I can wave my arms...

I can flop to the floor...

*(Pretend to be a puppet, moving as if held
together and moved by strings.)*

77

(Each child in turn picks an instrument and mimes playing it, singing the sound at the same time.)

I am the music man,
I come from down your way,
And I can play!

What can you play?

I can play the triangle.
Ding, ding, ding, ding, ding, ding, ding,
Ding, ding, ding,
Ding, ding, ding,
Ding, ding, ding, ding, ding, ding, ding,
Ding, ding, ding, ding, ding.

I can play the piano…
Dum, dum, dum, dum, dum, dumty
        dum…

78

I can play the recorder…
Toot, toot, toot, toot, toot, toot,
toot…

I can play the drums…
Boom, boom, boom, boom, boom,
boom, boom…

I can play the tambourine…
Shake-a, shake-a, shake-a, shake,
shake-a, shake, shake-a, shake…

79

INDEX